Willy Worm

Connie M. Campbell

authorHOUSE®

AuthorHouse™ LLC
1663 Liberty Drive
Bloomington, IN 47403
www.authorhouse.com
Phone: 1-800-839-8640

Published by AuthorHouse 07/28/2014

ISBN: 978-1-4969-3063-7 (sc)
ISBN: 978-1-4969-3062-0 (e)

Library of Congress Control Number: 2014914112

"CHANGE IS GOOD!"

"BEE A GOOD NEIGHBOR!"

"MAKE GOOD CHOICES!"

"BRING ON THE GOOD TIMES!"

"FREE WILLY'N!"

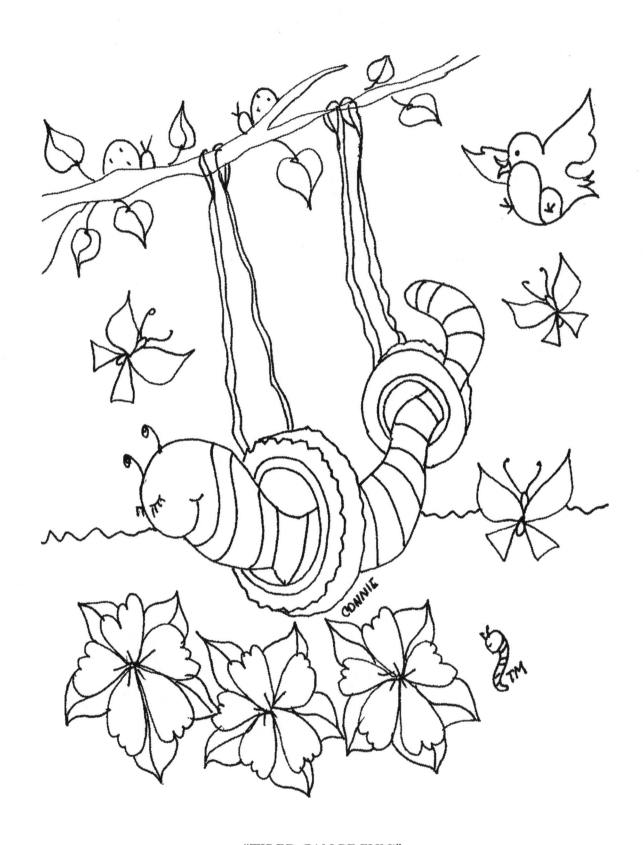

"TIRED CAN BE FUN!"

"...OH, BEAUTIFUL!"

"YOU CAN DO IT!"

"SHARING IS FUN!"

"YOU ARE THE WIND BENEATH MY WINGS!"

10

"SHORE LOVE MY FRIENDS!"

"VISITING FRIENDS IS FUN!"

"ENJOY YOUR VIEW!"

"MARCO!" "POLO!"

"WAKE UP, SLEEPY HEADS!"

"I CAN ROW A BOAT, CANOE?"

"BUG LIGHTS ATTRACT THE BEST!"

"IT'S YOUR MOVE!"

"THANK YOU FOR THE NIGHT AND FRIENDS!"

"EVERY STEP IS AN ADVENTURE!"

"ONE PLUS ONE IS TWO!" "I CAN COUNT ON YOU!"

"LOVE YOUR JOURNEY!"

"ALWAYS, WISHING WELL!"

"ROUND AND ROUND WE GO!"

"ALWAYS HELP A FRIEND!"

"PEEK-A-BOO!"

"PUMPKIN PATCH PALS!"

"KNOCK, KNOCK"… "WHO'S THERE?"

"RED FOR STOP, AMBER WAITS, GREEN FOR GO!"

"INGREDIENTS FOR FRIENDSHIP!"

"DIS-GUISE CUTE!"

"ALL THAT'S GOOD FOR YOU!"

"FIVE FUNNY FRIENDS!"

"THANKFUL FRIENDS!"

"FLOWERS NEED LOVE, TOO!"

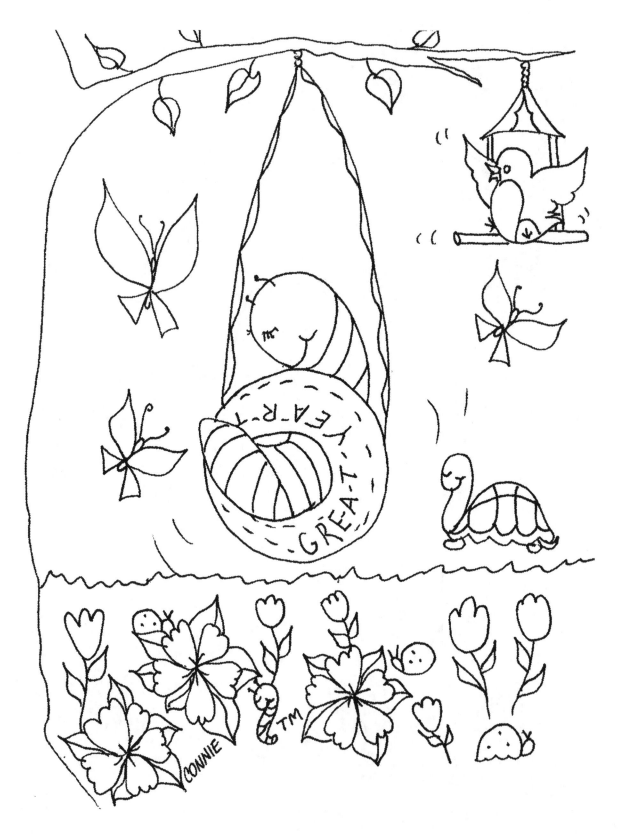

"JUST A SWINGIN'!"

"NAPS ARE NICE!"

"PAINT YOUR DAY HAPPY!"

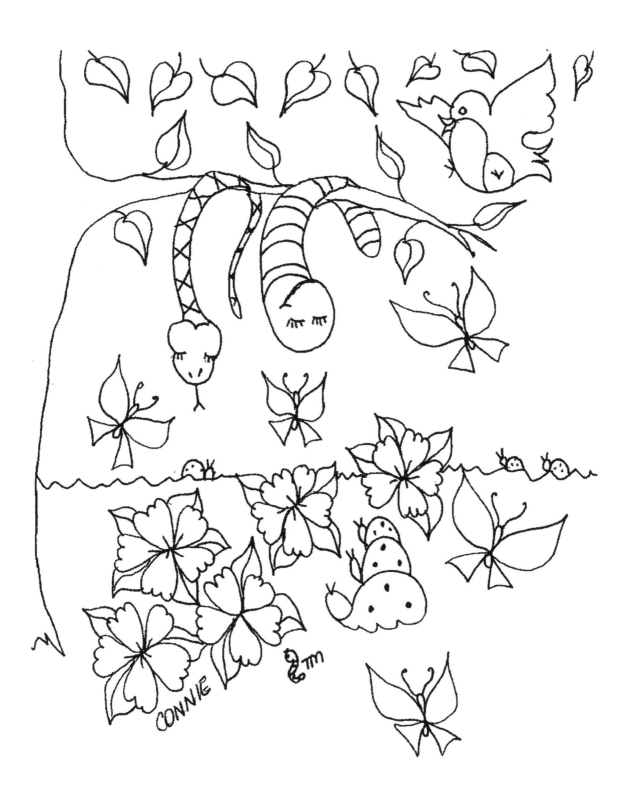

"HANGING WITH FRIENDS IS FUN!"

"COOL RIDE!"

"HAVE A "YEE-HAW" DAY!"

"FRIENDS SHARE ALL KINDS OF WEATHER!"

"ALWAYS KEEP IN TOUCH WITH FRIENDS!"

"WHEE, WE'RE HAVING FUN TOGETHER!"

"PULL UP A STOOL AND VISIT!"

"TIME JUST SLIDES AWAY!"

"YOU ARE THE BEST YOU, EVER!"

"STUDY WITH A SNACK!"

"PLAYING WITH FRIENDS IS FUN!"

"STRUM LOVERLY!"

Printed in the United States
By Bookmasters